(Continued from front flap)

that law was eternal. Holmes distrusted all absolutes, whether moral or legal, and said so frequently and vigorously.

If absolutes are largely discarded as guides to decision, the problem remains what general principles may be useful to members of the United States Supreme Court in determining the difficult questions of constitutional interpretation with which, after one hundred and seventy years, the court is still faced. This, Mr. Biddle examines in his concluding essay.

The Author—

Francis Biddle's life has been divided between active trial practice for twenty-five years in Philadelphia, and public service. A former Attorney General of the United States, he served Justice Holmes in the capacity of secretary when he was a youthful graduate of the Harvard Law School. During his distinguished career, he has been a judge on the Circuit Court of Appeals for the Third Circuit, Solicitor General of the United States, and a Member of the International Military Tribunal at Nürnberg. Mr. Biddle has written six books, one of which, a biography of Holmes, was the basis for ful Broadway play. He is a Bencher of the Inner London.

Justice Holmes, Natural Law,

and the Supreme Court

FRANCIS BIDDLE

JUSTICE HOLMES,

NATURAL LAW,

AND THE

SUPREME COURT

The Oliver Wendell Holmes Devise Lectures, 1960

THE MACMILLAN COMPANY NEW YORK 1961

FIRST PRINTING

The Macmillan Company, New York
Brett-Macmillan Ltd., Galt, Ontario

Printed in the United States of America

LIBRARY OF CONGRESS CATALOG CARD NUMBER: 61-10761

For HERBERT WECHSLER
with affection and gratitude for his help
with these lectures, and for much else,
during our twenty years of friendship.

Author's Note

THESE LECTURES, given at the University of Texas in December, 1960, at the invitation of the Permanent Committee for The Oliver Wendell Holmes Devise, although dealing with legal problems, are not intended primarily for members of the bar, but for a more general audience, who often cannot understand the approach of judges to the controversial problems of constitutional law which they are called on to "administer." The criticism of the Justice by Catholic scholars affords me not only an opportunity of discussing his views on the function and approach of appellate justices, but of inquiring what if any principles can guide them. This I have here attempted.

I want to express my thanks to the Library of Congress for affording me their admirable services.

Francis Biddle

Washington, D.C.
December, 1960

Contents

I

JUSTICE HOLMES

JUSTICE OLIVER WENDELL HOLMES

during his life, which was a very long one, and after his death enjoyed a reputation unparalleled by any American judge. Justice Cardozo said of him that of all the students of law and of human society Holmes was the greatest philosopher and seer of his age in the domain of jurisprudence, and "one of the greatest of any age." Two leading American historians, Morison and Commager, in *The Growth of the American Republic,* published two years after Justice Holmes's death, pronounced him "the most distinguished of all American jurists." In England Sir Frederick Pollock recognized his preeminence; and Lord Haldane (to whom I had a letter of introduction when the American Bar Association met in London in 1924—he was then Lord Chancellor) expressed to me the opinion that Holmes was a greater man than John Marshall.

A few years after Holmes's death, bitter attacks against him began in an obvious effort to destroy his reputation and to end his influence on contemporary American legal thinking. They came chiefly from exponents of natural law in the scholastic tradition, represented in the contemporary teaching of the Roman Catholic Church. Holmes did not believe in natural law or any other absolute, and said so a good many times without noticeable restraint. He included moralities and religious beliefs in the sweep of his skepticism, so that it was inevitable that those who did believe, and particularly those whose profession was based on the dogma of revelation, should sooner or later attack him. Holmes's approach was questioning, empirical, and pragmatic. It was postulated on the constant changes occurring in life that required similar changes in law—which is but one expression of life. It rejected absolutes, whether moral or legal. The other conception is based on principles, religious and philosophic, and cannot admit the existence of any decent, ordered society without their comforting support. To the believers in this doctrine the truth had been revealed, and they approach Justice Holmes with the zeal and intolerance of the crusading fanatic.

I shall in this lecture try to describe Holmes, not in any comprehensive way, but to give you a picture of what he was like, of how he felt and thought, in so far as this is useful to understand his beliefs and disbeliefs, especially as they affected his approach to the judicial process. I am among those who hold that his legal thinking was constructive as well as revolutionary. In my second lecture I shall examine the substance of the attacks, and inquire whether their authors knew what Holmes was talking about, and to what extent their shocked reactions were justified. And, since the conflict turned largely on the value of general principles in a system of law, I have thought it worth while in my last lecture to speculate as to the extent to which any general principles, however significant as creeds of a national purpose, may be useful to members of the Supreme Court in determining the difficult questions of constitutional interpretation, with which, after a hundred and seventy years, the Court is still faced.

MR. JUSTICE HOLMES was a remarkable human being—complex, full of apparent contradictions, a philosopher who considered all philosophic systems inadequate. "My intellectual furniture consists of an assortment of general propositions"—he wrote to his old friend Sir Frederick Pollock in 1904—"which grow fewer and more general as I grow older. I always say that the chief end of man is to frame them and that no general proposition is worth a damn." And he also knew that part of the business was to apply one's general mode of thought to the details.

He was New England to the marrow, cautious in his habits if not in his ideas, frugal, with something of the lurking Puritan within him. He had the robust health that so often goes with great vitality, temperance, and the habit of long rambles in the open air whenever there was a chance. He disliked extravagance and distrusted chronic moral exultation. When I was his secretary in Washington in 1911, he had to attend the obsequies of a Massachusetts dignitary for whom he had no particular esteem, and with a play of seriousness asked me whether I thought it all right if he wore his second-best overcoat to the funeral of a second-rate man. . . . Yet he was a citizen of a larger and riper world, a civilization which was his familiar intellectual country.

He was an immense reader in several languages, catholic in his tastes and wide in his range. I have in my possession a copy of a notebook which his executor, Mr. John Palfrey, gave to his secretaries after he died, in which Holmes listed the books he read each year. I was with him in 1911–1912, and for the former year he put down forty-nine books, among them Molière's *Le Tartuffe,* Dante's *Purgatorio* and *Paradiso,* Whitehead's *Introduction to Mathematics,* George Sand's *La Mare au Diable,* Graham Wallas's *Human Nature in Politics,* Keary's *Pursuit of Reason,* Stuart's *Cavalry in the Gettysburg Campaign,* by John S. Mosby, Plato's *Symposium* in the original Greek, Synge's *The Playboy of the Western World,* and Brieux's *La Petite Amie.* The year before he died he is off the Court and has plenty of leisure, enough for a hundred and sixteen books; and now E. Phillips Oppenheim, Noel Coward, and Agatha Christie mingle with Felix S. Cohen's *Ethical Systems and Legal Ideals* and Rexford G. Tugwell's *The Industrial Discipline and the Governmental Arts.* After he resigned from the Court at the age of ninety-one he would say that at last he had time to read P. G. Wodehouse and enjoy himself; but that he also had to fill in the gaps in his reading, for when he arrived at the Pearly Gates the first question that St. Peter would ask him was whether he had read *The Decline and Fall.* . . .

In June, 1922, Holmes wrote to Harold Laski, who had suggested some books for reading: "You mention for Beverly Farms, good God! Webb on this and that—and *Clothing Workers of Chicago.* My boy I mean to enjoy myself if I can—to get the unexpurgated *Pepys*—even read (going on) John Dewey's last in a philosophical way or Pound on Law but if you think that I am going to bother myself again before I die about social improvement, or read any of those stinking upward and onwarders—you err. I mean to have some good out of being old . . . I mean to go my own way, read what gives me pleasure, and leave the 'undone vast' for others." His writing was hard to decipher, and he added: "Those two words from Browning look a little like 'undone vest' . . . to be buttoned up by others. . . ."

Like most great men he remained close to the healthy strength of his own land, was never exiled from his American environment, even in the years when he thought the drift of politics and popular opinion was against the rules of the game on which he had been brought up—as he might have put it.

He was an aristocrat and a conservative. He did not prefer, he said, a world with a hundred million bores in it to one with ten. The fewer the people who do not contribute beauty or thought, the better. He had little sympathy with the sufferings and failures of mankind, and no urgent desire to change their lot. He thought that in the last analysis man rightly preferred his own interest to that of his neighbor, and did not believe in the Christian precept to love thy neighbor as thyself, which was the test of the meddling missionary: if men thought more about their jobs and less about themselves and their neighbors, they would accomplish more in the world.

He shared the general ideas that had been current when he was young, and he did not abandon them as he grew older. These made him skeptical of much of the social and economic legislation adopted after he came to Washington at the beginning of the twentieth century. He clung, for instance, to the argument of Malthus, the British curate who believed that population, unchecked by disease, war and poverty, would forever outdistance its means of subsistence, and remained pessimistic of possibilities of the future progress of mankind. Holmes wrote to Pollock in the summer of 1914 that he had been reading the *Nicomachean Ethics,* Descartes, Berkeley, Ricardo, and Malthus. Malthus both pleased him immensely, and left him sad: "A hundred years ago he busted fallacies that politicians and labor leaders still live on . . . Exposures amount to nothing when people want to believe."

Holmes kept coming back constantly to the same theme. He wished Malthus' teaching in its substance were more taken to heart. G. K. Chesterton in his *Victorian Age in Literature,* probably because he was a Catholic, had to be contemptuous of Malthus; and Holmes wrote to his young friend Harold Laski that he was reminded of what Lord Melbourne had said—it had tickled him:

"No one has more respect for the Christian religion than I have; but really, when it comes to intruding it into private life—"

All society rested on the death of men or on the prevention of the lives of a good many. So that when the Chief Justice assigned him the task of writing an opinion upholding the constitutionality of a Virginia law for sterilizing imbeciles he felt that he was getting near the first principle of real reform—although of course he didn't mean that the surgeon's knife was the ultimate symbol. . . . He was amused at some of the rhetorical changes in his opinion suggested by his associates, and purposely used "short and rather brutal words for an antithesis," that made them mad. In most cases the difficulty was rather with the writing than with the thinking. To put the case well and from time to time to hint at a vista was the job. . . .

This approach is characteristic of Holmes, and constantly reflected in his opinions—to keep the law fluid and the doors of the mind open. For pedestrian lawyers it was often unsatisfactory—they wanted everything defined and settled and turned into everlasting precedents.

Darwin's influence was strong on Holmes, and his theory of the survival of those who were fit to survive must have been constantly and passionately discussed in Dr. Holmes's house when Wendell was a growing lad and young man. *On the Origin of Species* had appeared when he was eighteen, and *The Descent of Man* in 1871, when he was thirty. Darwin led to Herbert Spencer, whom Holmes thought dull, with the ideals of a lower middle-class British Philistine, but who, with Darwin, he believed had done more than any other English writer to affect our whole way of thinking about the universe. All his life Holmes held to the survival of the strong, and did not disguise his view that the Sherman Act was a humbug, based on economic ignorance and incompetence, and that the Interstate Commerce Commission was not a fit body to be entrusted with rate making. However, as he said to Pollock, he was so skeptical about our knowledge of the goodness or badness of laws that he had no practical criticism except what the crowd wants. Personally he would bet that the crowd if it knew more wouldn't want what it does.

In my brief life of Justice Holmes * I commented on certain of his economic theories; and John W. Davis, who was Solicitor General of the United States from 1913 to 1918, when he read it, wrote to me that, after argument in an antitrust case, he walked away from the Court with the Justice. "Mr. Solicitor," asked Holmes, "how many more of these economic policy cases have you got?" "Quite a basketful," Davis answered airily. "Well," said the Justice, "bring 'em on and we'll decide 'em. Of course I know, and every other sensible man knows, that the Sherman law is damned nonsense, but if my country wants to go to hell, I am here to help it."

Holmes believed that ideas had more influence on the human race in the long run than action, and that Kant had a firmer hold on greatness than Napoleon. But Holmes himself had so much vitality, and admiration for its display by others, that he held that John D. Rockefeller was not entitled to a front seat in Heaven, because all his life he had been so busy grubbing and adding and toiling and saving that he never stopped to consider what he was doing or where he was going; but in spite of this he should be given one of the rear seats. . . . When Holmes, who was then Chief Justice of the Massachusetts Supreme Court, formulated his philosophy in a speech to the Boston Bar Association by saying that *life is action, the use of one's powers,* his old friend William James was disappointed: to celebrate mere vital excitement, *joie de vivre,* and to make it systematic, was childish, "especially when one is a Chief Justice."

* Scribner's, 1941.

BUT THE striking fact was not that Holmes's thought followed the furrow plowed by Darwin and Herbert Spencer and John Stuart Mill, and that he championed private competition with as much enthusiasm as some of his associates on the United States Supreme Court from whom he so frequently dissented—Van Devanter, Sutherland, Pierce Butler, McReynolds—but that he refused to let his preferences (other men were apt to call them convictions) interfere with his judicial decisions. He was convinced that one who administers constitutional law should multiply his skepticisms to avoid heading into vague words like *liberty,* and reading into law his private convictions or the prejudices of his class. The steadily held determination to keep his own views isolated from his professional work is aptly shown by his famous remark in the *Lochner* case—"the Fourteenth Amendment does not enact Mr. Herbert Spencer's *Social Statics.* . . . A constitution is not intended to embody a particular economic theory, whether of paternalism and the organic relation of the citizen to the State or of *laissez faire.*" He remembered what Marshall had said, that it was a *constitution* he was expounding, and not a document evoked by a particular doctrine for a particular time. For, above all, he was conscious, unlike most conservatives, too often bent on recapturing their youth and framing the present within the past, of the constant flux and change of the world, and the streaming pressure of fresh thought and new invention.

Like many traditionalists, who prefer to preserve the *status quo,* Holmes had little understanding of or sympathy with the economic outlook of the growing "paternalism" that was beginning to curb the excesses of laissez faire and banish the cruelties of the industrial revolution which had taken place since he was a student.

(*10*)

Economics was not his métier; but his bias toward unfettered competition did not prevent him, as Justice Frankfurter has noted, from enforcing statutes based upon economic theories that he did not share. He had his own theories. One which he held particularly dear, perhaps because he imagined that it was his discovery, was that we should think in terms of consumption instead of terms of ownership, so that the real problem was not who owns but who consumes the stream of goods. He believed that most men think dramatically and not quantitatively, and that we are apt to contrast the palace with the hovel, and dinner at Sherry's with the workingman's dinner pail, whereas the point was in the general flow of consumption. He came back to this idea continually in letters and in at least one opinion, without apparently considering the power involved in ownership, and its effect on distribution.

Yet, influenced as he was by doctrines that were current during his youth, and had become a religious dogma among many by the time he began his long career in the United States Supreme Court in 1902, Holmes was interested in the new ideas current in the world, largely because they challenged the self-confident certainty of his own views—vigorous disagreement provoked thought. He did not particularly dread the new ideas, like many of his contemporaries, or think that the world would come to an end if they were accepted. But if he avoided translating his own preferences into the law, he could fight vigorously to keep his associates on the Supreme Court from insisting on the application of theirs, particularly some of the older generation of judges who "regarded a difference of opinion as a cockfight and often left a good deal to be desired in point of manners." He hesitated to dissent, but could do so with eloquent obstinacy when he got the "blood of controversy in [his] neck."

He felt it a misfortune for a judge to read his conscious or unconscious sympathy with one side or the other, and forget that what seemed to him to be first principles were believed by half his fellow men to be wrong. "When twenty years ago," he said in one of his infrequent addresses, "a vague terror went over the earth and the word socialism began to be heard, I thought and still think that fear was translated into doctrines that had no proper place in the Constitution or the common law. Judges are apt to be naif, simple-minded men, and they need something of Mephistopheles."

The old boy had something of Mephistopheles in himself— the Mephistopheles who summoned Marlowe and Shakespeare, Fletcher and Goethe and Thomas Mann; and who, after giving Dr. Faustus twenty-four glorious years of youth and love, carried him off at night between the 23rd and 24th of October, 1538. In Holmes the Mephistophelean attributes were an amused arrogance, a rebellious iconoclasm—he would reach out to pull down the sanctities if they showed signs of interfering with the earth-born—and a delight in paradoxes—there was nothing like a good paradox to take the scum off your mind. He wrote to his friend Lewis Einstein that morals were a contrivance of man to take himself seriously. He liked to talk with a flourish about wicked French novels —"now for some French indecency to restore the tone of my mind" he confided to Einstein—and to suggest that if only he had time to indulge in capers there was nothing that would please him more. In the event he was an extremely abstemious man, whose habit was to smoke two cigars a day—big ones—and three on great occasions, such as the night of March 8, 1921, when Mrs. Holmes gave him a surprise birthday party attended by as many of his former secretaries as she could collect. . . . If you did not think like a devil, he liked to say, you could not touch the deepest complexities of the absolute.

One Monday, he remarked to Harold Laski, that after conference and Court he whisked home and landed on a reception (the ladies of the Court were at home on Mondays) where he lit on an unknown dame with a southern accent, and the devil set his tongue loose. He told her that abuses were the parents of the exquisite, which vanished from the country with wine, that he loathed most of the things in favor of which he decided, and that you couldn't have a people like the Greeks except on a basis of some kind of slavery. "Wouldn't that have made some headlines if she had been a female reporter?"

HOLMES'S LIFE may conveniently be divided into three stages. First came his three years in the Union Army, years of intense and uninterrupted action, without thought of the future, without books, with no plan ahead and no end of it all, at a time when he was very young (he enlisted at nineteen) and impressionable, and the impact and disillusionment of war was to haunt him and shape his character for the rest of his life. Then there was a period of scholarship and speculation, of thought without action: the Harvard Law School, his work on the twelfth edition of Kent's *Commentaries,* lecturing on constitutional law and jurisprudence at Harvard, editing the *American Law Review,* and finally the brilliant historical investigation that culminated in *The Common Law* in 1881. The book became famous all over the world, and the London *Spectator* (which almost never noticed the work of an American author) hailed it as the most original work of legal speculation since the publication of Sir Henry Maine's *Ancient Law,* which had appeared in 1861. The third period began with Holmes's appointment on the Massachusetts Supreme Court when he was forty-one, and ended with thirty years on the Supreme Court of the United States—years which in a broad sense were filled with action as well as reflection, for the work was that of a statesman as well as of a thinker, and his decisions shaped the development of the country no less, perhaps, than those made by the men who had been elected to govern.

His eyes had been opened by the war to see life as it was, not as the politicians or poets described it, but drifting and meaning-less, the dream forgotten, faith destroyed. As his biographer Mark De Wolfe Howe has suggested, he saw a number of his convictions crumble when they clashed with the impact of reality, and the convictions of others stand firm. War forced Holmes to examine the bases of his own moral assumptions (that centered around the abolition of slavery), and deepened his skepticism when he realized that many of the young officers who were his friends were cynical about the "holy crusade" and fought and died for a cause which they inwardly rejected. Skepticism led to tolerance, and he could no longer continue to believe that his own conceptions of what was right and what was evil had any cosmic significance. From war he had learned not only to distrust his own beliefs, but to respect those of others.

And yet he could combine this new-found skepticism with the old enthusiasm of faith which had led him to join the Twentieth Massachusetts. Just as this faith balanced his doubts about the ab-solutes that lay like shapes of dreams outside the experience of a world you could touch and feel, so an echo of romance hovered be-hind his rational outlook, and transcended it, particularly when he thought of the war, as he so often did, in which three times he had been wounded. War was also horrible because it was dull. "I re-member just before the battle of Antietam," he wrote to his young friend Dr. John C. H. Wu in 1923, "thinking and perhaps saying to a brother officer that it would be easy after a comfortable break-fast to come down the steps of one's house pulling on one's gloves and smoking a cigar to get on a horse and charge a battery up Beacon Street, while the ladies wave handkerchiefs from a balcony. But the reality was to pass a night on the ground in the rain with your bowels out of order and then after no particular breakfast to wade a stream and attack the enemy. That is life." But there was more to life than war, and more to war than cold and hunger and dysentery.

Out of the loss of faith in a shared belief in the cause of right-eousness for which it was supposed that his own side was fighting, out of that disillusion he could create and hold for the rest of his life a vision of the romance of war that for him was ennobling, for it had drawn brave men together. He needed it to live down his bitter disappointment. He tried to outline this vision, uncertain yet stirring, in a Memorial Day address thirty years after the Civil War had ended. He did not know, he said, what was true; he did not know the meaning of the universe: "But in the midst of doubt, in the collapse of creeds, there is one thing I do not doubt, that no man who lives in the same world with most of us can doubt, and that is that the faith is true and adorable which leads a soldier to throw away his life in obedience to a blindly accepted duty, in a cause which he little understands, in a plan of campaign of which he has no notion, under tactics of which he does not see the use."

The passage has often been criticized, and to a later generation, not raised on the illusion of the romance of war, there is something shocking about the implication that it is a noble thing to be killed in a war without a purpose. But for Holmes this was, as Mark Howe has suggested, his effort to justify, so far as he could, the sacrifice of so many of his friends, men who had fought next to him, but who had been cynical about the whole business, a justification which could not find itself in reason. And this stir of mystery which now and then rose when he pondered a universe that he could never know, kept fresh the insights that might have turned arid in an intellect limited to the reaches of reason.

WHEN HOLMES LEFT the army and went to live in the garret of the house that his father had built at 296 Beacon Street in Boston, overlooking the Charles River, he was constantly in the atmosphere of his father's empirical approach to medicine under the impact of the new scientific methods which had begun to be felt.

Lord Coke had said that reason was embodied in the life of the law. Holmes thought otherwise—and, since it shows the touchstone of his thinking, I must quote the much-quoted passage from the opening paragraph of *The Common Law:* "The life of the law has not been logic: it has been experience. The felt necessities of the time, the prevalent moral and political theories, intuitions of public policy, avowed or unconscious, even the prejudices which judges share with their fellow-men, have had a good deal more to do than the syllogism in determining the rules by which men should be governed. The law embodies the story of a nation's development through many centuries, and it cannot be dealt with as if it contained only the axioms and corollaries of a book of mathematics. In order to know what it is, we must know what it has been, and what it tends to become." The substance of the law, Holmes continued, corresponds at any given time with what is understood to be convenient. That involves continual change, and there can be no eternal order.

This new and startling viewpoint was radically opposed to the accepted convictions of American judges and lawyers who, long after the publication of *The Common Law*—which had followed the same direction as *Ancient Law,* but with new insights—continued to believe what Blackstone had written, that judges were not delegated to pronounce new law but to find and expound the old. In spite of Holmes's immense influence on American legal thinking, the comforting formula that law was eternal still persisted, and Calvin Coolidge could blandly announce that "men do not make laws, they do but discover them."

If you clung to the tradition of Blackstone and President Coolidge, the test (theoretically at least) was very simple, for morals too were eternal and did not change, just as natural law is basic and immutable. "This law of nature," Blackstone wrote, "being co-eval with mankind and dictated by God himself, is of course superior in obligation to any other. It is binding over all the globe, in all the countries, and at all times: no human laws are of any validity, if contrary to this; and such of them as are valid derive all their force, and all their authority, mediately or immediately, from this original." No natural law exponent could have asked for a more embracing pronouncement. But the learned commentator immediately added that in order to apply this to the particular exigencies of each individual, it is still necessary to have recourse to reason, "whose office it is to discover . . . what the law of nature directs in every circumstance of life." This is still the doctrine of the natural law lawyer.

Blackstone had enormous influence on American legal thinking, and his doctrines became embedded in the opinions of American judges, not so much as guides to judgment, which they professed to be, but as resounding ethical justifications for decisions already taken, so as to give them the authority of theological verities, which obviously cannot be analyzed but which carry the solid reference of time and faith in their wake.

It was against this static concept, blocking change and making law curiously outmoded and inexpressive of life, that Holmes's stalwart genius reacted. His scholarship searched the reason for the rules that, as he said, like the clavicle of the cat, had become obsolete; he discarded the legal phrases that had so long dammed up thinking; and his sense of the changing and often contradictory needs of human beings made a link between history and the functional world of which law is but one expression.

IT HAS BEEN suggested that Holmes was full of contradictions, that he was skeptical of everything, yet had much of the poet and mystic about him, and that at the end he began to show uncertainty about his own rejection of the verities. But this view of him is too compartmentalized. He had both skepticism and faith, the combination making him what Judge Jerome Frank has called a completely adult jurist; and he clung to his own beliefs to the end.

Catherine Drinker Bowen, collecting material in Washington before writing *Yankee From Olympus,* said to Mr. Justice Brandeis: "People like to call Holmes a sceptic. . . . Did you ever hear Holmes express a conviction about mankind, a philosophic conviction?" Brandeis thought for a moment. "Holmes had a conviction," he answered, "that man should be free in a large way. He was a great liberator. He was a great emancipator."

His doubts gave him that freedom, with the conviction that it was basic to understanding. They emancipated him from the dogmatic assumptions of his profession, as well as from domination by his personal prejudices, and brought tolerance, the mark of a civilized man. Holmes recognized that in those prejudices lay the faith which he cherished, but would not inflict on others. As a young man he had realized that there can be no such thing as total skepticism. He copied in his notebook a passage from a book by Edward Caird, *The Social Philosophy and Religion of Comte:* "All criticism of the whole system of things to which we belong is, from a truly 'relative' point of view, irrational. For the critic and the standard by which he criticizes, cannot be separated from that system. It has often been pointed out that a logical scepticism cannot be universal. Doubt must rest on a basis of certitude, or it will destroy itself. But it is not less true, though it is less frequently noticed, that all criticism of the world, while it detects evil in particular, implies an ultimate optimism. For if such criticism pretends to be more than the utterance of the tastes and wishes of an individual, it must claim to be the expression of an objective principle—a principle which, in spite of all appearances to the contrary, is realizing itself in the world." Holmes was struck by the passage, and added a comment: "I have been saying for 20 years that the sceptic must be an optimist because to be a pessimist (in the philosophic sense) postulates a standard independent of the universe by which to condemn it—Oct. 6/85." He then changed his comment to read *the sceptic cannot be a pessimist*. The words evidently tickled his sense of irony; and added, underscored: *For possible collection of solider writings*.

His speculations were based on his first postulate—that he was a part of the universe—the universe was not in his belly. That led to the second revealing discovery (for any man) that he was not God, which was the beginning of an enlightened skepticism. How can a man take himself seriously enough to attribute cosmic importance to his thought? Of course he didn't mean being serious in his living and functioning, but in believing that he knew the riddle of the universe. He himself could experience the universe, but could never understand it, outside that necessary presumption that it existed, or know whether it had any direction or purpose or deity. It showed no signs of caring for him, or for any particular human being; it suggested no standard, no moral law, no sense of the ethical values commonly ascribed to it. But *his* world (it was no one else's, for there was no way of fusing experience) was warm and real, and not without idealism.

He grew fond of this mysterious universe, liked to call it the Cosmos, and to make jokes about it. For there it was, and there was no use shaking your fist at it if you didn't like it, any more than complaining about the rain or cold or death. You could feel them, but couldn't alter them by complaints—it was like shaking your fist at the sky, like Bertrand Russell, a sentimentalist disguised as a skeptic, who hadn't given up the notion that absolute truth was still attainable.

But if Holmes could not discourse about the universe except to describe its indifference, he had faith in life as he lived it, and zest for his own realities. Life was an end in itself, and the only question as to whether it was worth living was whether you had enough of it. The doubts of Henry Adams, Holmes's friend, were not religious, but evidenced a mistrust of the value of contemporary living, with his aesthetic sensibility translated into a contempt for the crude, raw, careless throb of America—a turmoil which Holmes met with his head up and a beating pulse. But then Henry Adams would have been depressed by any civilization in which he lived. Adams, Holmes thought, had the gift of turning all life to ashes. Holmes was not without a sense of the destructive quality of such an attitude; and when once he was developing his doubts to a younger friend, he was struck by the other's comment that Holmes seemed to express himself in fears rather than in faith.

And Holmes was intensely American, with the friendly and humorous outlook of the average American. Alice James, who lived for years with her brother Henry in England to try to recover her failing health, noted in her diary a remark of "W.H." (Holmes). The torpid A. G. Sedgwick, Miss James wrote, told her one day that, after handing a telegram to the clerk (presumably in Boston), he, Sedgwick, had asked whether the message was plain, and the answer had been, "Plain, but peculiar." Sedgwick, a proper Bostonian, thought this very bad manners; but O.W.H. said that the absence of such possibilities was what made one homesick in Europe. . . .

HOLMES'S LIFE was grounded on hard, lonely, unending work. He believed nothing that came easily was worth having, and it was important to get life by the throat rather than by the tail. He loved the country for which he had fought and had been wounded, and left to the United States the residue of his modest fortune. At the fiftieth reunion of his class at Harvard, on June 28, 1911, he told his old classmates that he had learned in the regiment that the best service we could do for our country and for ourselves was to see, so far as we may, and to feel the great forces that are behind every detail, for that makes all the difference between great action and small; to hammer out as compact and solid a piece of work as we can, to try to make it first rate, and to leave it unadvertised. Man is born a predestined idealist, for he is born to act. Life is painting a picture, not doing a sum. To act is to affirm the worth of an end, and to persist in affirming the worth of an end is to make an ideal. Then all his New England background comes out: "Pleasures do not make happiness . . . and the root of joy as of duty is to put all one's powers toward some great end. Life," he continued, "is a roar of bargain and battle, but in the very heart of it there rises a mystic spiritual tone that gives meaning to the whole. It transmutes the dull details into romance. It reminds us that our only but wholly adequate significance is as parts of the unimaginable whole. It suggests that even while we think that we are egotists we are living to ends outside ourselves."

I have quoted this passage to show how little the word "skeptic" covers the depth and significance of Holmes's nature. It is an important part of him, but not the whole. And just as he could not escape his New England instincts of thrift and caution, so he could not altogether cut the thread which tied him to the great New England divines, from Increase Mather with his stern Calvinism to Emerson, a Unitarian who resigned from his Church, and who, as Holmes said of him, had been the firebrand of his youth. Was not Holmes, in truth, the last of the Puritans?

I stress the spiritual and moral side of Justice Holmes, because he is attacked for being a frank cynic, a materialist without morals, caring for nothing but force. He did not believe in any system of ethics; systems to him were as meaningless as all other absolutes, although he could not resist the temptation of philosophic speculation, of *divine gossip* as he called it. That he was without a conventional set of fixed principles—how many of us could recite on our own creed?—did not prevent him, as we have seen, from preaching the virtues to which he clung, whenever he was asked to speak in public. These addresses, "chance utterances of faith and doubt . . . little fragments of my fleece that I have left upon the hedges of life," as he referred to them, were few and far between over the thirty years they covered, but, coupled with his letters and opinions, carry the whole range and complexity of his thinking.

He continually turned back to his Civil War experience, not only to remember its sacrifices, but because it had been for him *action and passion,* and it was required of a man that he should share the action and passion of his time at peril of being judged not to have lived. That belief in living hard, in using everything that was in him, in following his vision to the end, he never lost. Part of life, he wrote, is to feel a direction for effort and to persevere with faith—"that at least is my case. If I were dying my last words would be: Have faith and pursue the unknown end."

In 1913 he spoke to younger men at a dinner of the Harvard Law School Association in New York. Like everything he said in public, this address was compressed into half a dozen paragraphs, and could not have taken more than ten minutes to deliver. Law, he told these lawyers, embodies beliefs that have triumphed in the battle of ideas, and then have translated themselves into action. . . . As he grew older he admitted to what perhaps were an old man's apprehensions—he was seventy-two and would sit on the Court for almost another twenty years—that competition from new races would cut deeper than workingmen's disputes and would test whether we could hang together and could fight. . . . But he did not lose hope, and thought it probable that civilization somehow would last as long as he cared to look ahead—perhaps with smaller numbers, but perhaps also bred to greatness and splendor by science. He ventured the thought "that man, like the grub that prepares a chamber for the winged thing it never has seen but is to be—that man may have cosmic destinies that he does not understand." He spoke of his faith "in a universe not measured by our fears, a universe that has thought and more than thought inside of it."

AT FIRST GLANCE Justice Holmes seems full of inconsistencies and contradictions: his faith and skepticism; his personal arrogance, and the humility with which he approaches his own credo; his Puritanism—and his taste for improprieties coupled with his impulse to shock; his distrust of theories and his habit of indulging in them. But when we examine these dissimilarities more closely, they resolve themselves into a complex but integrated nature. He was all of a piece. And the characteristics which I have described are reflected in his approach to law, so that it was to be expected that when the attacks came they should be aimed at the man as well as the legal thinker. The two cannot be separated.

The legal thinking sprang from an historical view of law. Its life was found not in *a priori* theorizing but in man's experiments with his own way of living. Law, like life, was constantly changing. Since law was based on the life of the community, it reflected the community's moral outlook—but law and morals were not the same thing. The role of the judge was to keep his own preferences out of his decisions, and to discover and follow, so far as he could, the substance of the law which, at any given time, corresponded with what was understood to be convenient. Therefore the American Constitution must be thought of as an instrument intended to fit an organic and growing society.

II

THE ATTACK ON JUSTICE HOLMES

THE ATTACKS ON JUSTICE HOLMES

were stirred into life by the publication of his letters a few years after his death—there was hardly enough in the opinions and speeches to shock the well-bred ear of the average man; and the priests, who wrote most of the criticism, must have spent many hours combing the letters to sustain their view that here was a modern antichrist worthy of their mettle. The Justice's admirers came to his defense, but only here and there, and with dignity and caution, as if the charges were not worth answering, and it was simply a matter of misunderstanding their hero. It would be pointless, however, to get into this battle of words in the law journals, in itself hardly an engrossing subject, were it not for the fact that it represents not merely misunderstanding, but two points of view about the law and the proper approach to its application that are fundamentally opposed, and touch the roots of its life.

The first letters published (in 1936) were to John C. H. Wu, a young Chinese student with a solemn philosophic bent, who would later be a judge of the Shanghai Provisional Court. The letters to Sir Frederick Pollock—the English scholar descended from David Pollock, a saddler to George III, whom Holmes called "one of the very most learned men I ever saw in any age"—appeared in 1941, the correspondence covering a friendship that lasted for almost sixty years. Finally came the letters to Harold Laski (1916 to 1935), an obscure, frail young Englishman, instructor in government at Harvard, who was taken by Felix Frankfurter, then teaching at the Harvard Law School, to see Holmes at Beverly Farms in the summer of 1916.

Holmes's correspondence was enormous—many of his letters are still unpublished—he wrote everything in longhand, and he spent as much pains on his letters as he did on his opinions, and short occasional addresses to a group of veterans or a meeting of the bar. I would not deny that he had an eye cocked for posterity, particularly in the letters; but the chief reason for his concentrated and minute exertions was his lifelong habit of reaching for perfection, not unrelated to his deeply ingrained way of never laying down a book he had begun—if you start something you must finish it. It was therefore like him to exclaim, "How one hates a book while one is reading it!"

Holmes's letters to Pollock are more restrained, more sober than what he wrote Laski, and display more legal scholarship, as if to show his friend that since he became a judge he had not given up reading what was being said about the nature and sources of law. The letters to Laski carry the wit and insight and charm of his talk; Laski is indiscreet—and brilliant. Everything about Holmes is there; and one feels that the younger man's broad culture and omnivorous reading, even allowing for his boasts about it—"I can't believe that you read all the books you mention," Holmes bursts out, *he* couldn't swallow books like oysters—and the fact that

Laski's point of view was teasingly alien to the Justice's challenged him to do his utmost in the long-drawn intellectual duel.

Holmes said what he liked in the letters—he must have sometimes felt penned in among his brethren in Washington—which range over a broad field of life and law, of literature and philosophy, of the beliefs and doubts of men. They are written with lucidity and concision, without consciousness of the need to exercise discretion which the opinions and public talks necessarily imposed. Of course he repeats himself; and the repetitions show how little the ideas he held most closely, the "can't helps," as he called them, changed over the years. I don't mean to say that these beliefs could not have been found in the opinions and his occasional addresses; but they lack the atmosphere of casual ease in which friends indulge when they do not fear being quoted, at least until the lapse of time takes from their talk the sting of the contemporary. Holmes must have felt a boyish pleasure of indulging in expressions, which, particularly to the canonical, were more shocking than the ideas which they were intended to convey.

FOLLOWING THE UPHEAVAL of a great war, or of profound economic and scientific changes, traditions break down and the truths of yesterday are no longer accepted; men look for spiritual guidance outside their own limited experience, and grasp at religion to reestablish their sense of direction. Today is such a time. Side by side with the present mood of violence and despair there is a reaction against cynicism, a demand for the comfort of the mystical, a desire to be reassured and to be instructed. "The insecurities of our age today," Reinhold Niebuhr has observed, "strongly tempt this generation, not to the utopianism of yesterday but to flight into any kind of storm cellar of religious security, whether this be Biblicism . . . or emphasis on the uniqueness of the church." It is not surprising, therefore, that natural law—which in the past has promised so much—has had a revival in the Catholic law schools, somewhat doctrinaire, in an endeavor to clarify and to justify its tenets.

Among those who drew their moral sustenance from natural law, Holmes's reputation must have suffered under the assaults of certain Roman Catholic priests teaching in Jesuit law schools, whose charges I shall presently examine. I do not believe that their extreme views and lack of restraint in the manner of expressing them represent the thought of Jesuits as a body, many of them enlightened legal scholars. Though of course they accept the principles of natural law, these principles do not differ greatly from the ethical concepts of Protestants, or of members of other denominations, or of men of good will who happen to be freethinkers. One does not have to be a cleric to be an upright man, and most thoughtful lawyers talk the same language. Yet several of my friends, who are prominent Catholic lawyers and judges, and whose opinions and views I respect, have gathered the impression from reading the law-review articles that we shall consider, that Holmes was a cynic, who thought of law as nothing but the application of force; that he believed that morals, basically conceived, were but the expression of individual taste, and had nothing to do with law; and that he held that the proper function of a judge was to carry out what the majority had already decided, whether it was right or wrong.

I do not think that Holmes's ultimate place in history, or the tradition that has grown up around the nation's memory of him as an heroic and noble figure, will be affected by these onslaughts, sometimes highly personal and ungoverned. Yet it seems to me appropriate to meet them—they have not, I think, been adequately answered outside law-school journals. That I loved and admired Justice Holmes makes it difficult for me to resist this opportunity to talk about him and his detractors. But this is not merely a matter of coming to the defense of a great man whom little men are trying to pull down. Holmes's contribution to law—his insistence on examining objectively the facts which explain its life and its direction—involves keeping open the doors of the mind in a world which increasingly, I feel, is closing about us. The attacks are leveled against the emancipation of law from superstition—a task to which everything in Holmes was dedicated.

I DO NOT propose to define natural law, or to discuss its often contradictory tenets. But it is essential to know in the most general way some of the claims of natural law which the critics of Justice Holmes had in mind in order to understand why he rejected them, and the reasons he was attacked for doing so. This rejection, as we have seen, was leveled at all moral absolutes, particularly if they were confused with law.

There have been many schools of natural law, which is speculative and dogmatic, and its range has been used to cover the whole field of morals. It is said, for instance, that the International Military Tribunal at Nuremberg applied natural law. It did not; but punished what the charter, under which it operated, designated as *crimes against humanity*. It may be replied that this reference was itself taken from natural law; but that is true only in the most general sense. The phrase was an expression of the reaction of the conscience of the community against evils which seemed so shocking that they must be considered "crimes." That is the way in which the common law of crime largely developed, and many early crimes were not spelled out in any statute, or in the decree of a sovereign. Like the doctrine of equity, natural law has had marked influence on English common law, although it is not the same as common law, and has never absorbed it.

Since the substance of natural law is a statement of what is thought to be moral, it is not surprising to find it invoked on both sides when controversy arises. In our Declaration of Independence the assertion that all men are endowed by their Creator with certain unalienable rights is drawn from natural law; yet such a ringing and noble expression of faith did not prevent Americans from writing slavery into their Constitution; or Southerners from claiming in the Civil War that slavery was sanctified by the laws of nature. Albert Dicey, the English scholar, said of natural law that it had often been a name for the dictates of expediency. It has noticeably influenced American thinking, and many of its pronouncements are indistinguishable from the democratic outlook of normal Americans. Generally speaking it is today not thought of as a church doctrine but as the assertion of certain general rights to be taken for granted: men have a *right* to liberty; they have a *right* to happiness; they have a *right* to fair trial. Some hold that men are born with these rights; others that God gives them to men. Few pause to ask who enforces the rights, and how, and whether rights that cannot be enforced are in fact inalienable.

Often, natural law is spoken of as that body of moral behavior practiced in the community by men of good will over a long period of years, so that it has come to be universally accepted as a broad canon of decencies on which most men agree. Again, where such generality is assumed, awkward questions are forgotten or overlooked. Does natural law exist in a civilization dominated by Communist dogma? If not, was it ended at a certain time and place, or does it still hover, as it were, "a brooding omnipresence in the sky"—to use Holmes's apt phrase—which will descend to earth when the time is ripe; or is there a natural law of Communism which has its own set of dogmatic absolutes? Such questions are by no means irrelevant, as the kind of natural law espoused by the Roman Catholic Church claims that its precepts are universal and eternal.

THE CONCENTRATED CRITICISM of Holmes began in 1941 when the Reverend Francis E. Lucey, S.J., a writer who theretofore had been, comparatively speaking, unknown, published an article in *Social Science* called "Jurisprudence and the Future Social Order." Other priests joined in the attack, chiefly in the legal periodicals of the Catholic law schools, but Father Lucey was in the front ranks, continually coming back to do battle, distinguished from his associates by his intemperate language, the increasing length of each article, and his admirable collection of Holmes's aphorisms, largely drawn from the letters, to prove his points. Father John C. Ford, S.J., in the same year addressed the annual convention of the Jesuit Philosophical Association on "The Fundamentals of Holmes' Juristic Philosophy." A month later the Reverend William J. Kenealy, S.J., Dean of the Boston College Law School, at the celebration of the Red Mass in that city, using for the title of his pronouncements "The Majesty of the Law," indicated his conviction that the alien philosophies of Kant, Hume, Herbert Spencer, John Stuart Mill, Hobbes, Marx, and now Holmes were "cutting away at the foundations of American jurisprudence," and might "topple the superstructure which we are proud and happy to call our American Way of Life." It is not inaccurate to suggest that Father Kenealy's exhortations were more rhetorical than lucid.

There were other, similar attacks, and a debate in the *American Bar Association Journal,* which stirred up a lively controversy among lawyers for a brief moment of time. Fred Rodell of the Yale Law School, and Mark Howe of Harvard, wrote law-review articles contrasting Holmes's views with those of the Jesuits, which drew blood from Father Lucey, for he rushed back to the attack—he did not think much of these two professors, though Rodell was "not quite as smooth and snide as Howe."

The charges against Holmes are about the same in all the articles and addresses: he was a skeptic and cynic who believed in no God and had no principles; he considered that law was nothing but the use of force, and that might makes right; he discarded all absolutes, including natural law, and defined truth as the vote of the majority; and he described morals as nothing but a curb on the normal human inclination to get your feet in the trough.

AS I SUGGESTED, Holmes's skepticism was by no means complete, but was balanced and humanized by a sturdy belief in the things he cared about. He shared with other men of his time acceptance of the ordinary decencies—courage, abstinence, truth, a sane mind in a healthy body, honesty, and loyalty. These did not differ in any marked degree from those which these priests acknowledged. But Holmes would not call them eternal because he was a philosophic as well as a religious skeptic. His detractors could not concede that anyone who rejected God could be a good man.

Nor did Holmes hold that the essence of law was physical force, as Father Ford asserted, trying hard to understand this terrifying unbeliever whom he could not help admiring; and Father Ford had no grounds for surmising that from this it followed that Holmes believed that might makes right. What Holmes did say—and repeated in various ways—was that law was a *statement of the circumstances in which the public force will be brought to bear upon men through the courts.* On reflection Father Ford might have accepted such a statement as a commonplace. When Holmes talked of law he always meant the same thing—the law that lawyers practice and judges declare, and from which human beings suffer; the law that permits a policeman to shoot an escaping felon, or a sheriff to manacle a kidnaper, or a judge to send a man to jail for refusing to testify. And in that sense law—what we call positive law—is based on force, and can hardly be said to exist unless it can be enforced. To Holmes law, like sovereignty, was a fact. The only external limit that he could see to the power of the lawmaker was the limit of power as a question of fact. This had nothing to do with the difficulty of finding out who the sovereign was, or the tacitly recognized *de facto* limits of the power of the most absolute sovereign (or state) that ever was. So when he talked of law he talked like a cynic. He didn't "care a damn if twenty professors" told him that a decision was not law if he knew that the courts would enforce it. When he spoke of the lawmaking power he meant concurrence of all the necessary organs of government in putting an enactment into execution.

Holmes was not talking about Father Ford's absolutes, floating somewhere as ideals in men's minds, essences of what law should be (but hardly ever is). So Holmes said—and Father Ford held up his hands—"Just so far as the aid of the public force is given a man, he has a legal right, and this right is the same whether his claim is founded in righteousness or iniquity." Is not this carefully exact? Holmes is not discussing the problem of what makes law, or inspires it, or influences its direction, or what it should be; he is telling us in hard, clear, definite language what it is: "Law being a practical thing, must found itself on actual forces."

Father Ford had been brought up, theologically speaking, on St. Thomas Aquinas and his doctrine that *all* law is based on natural law implanted by God in man. But he would not, I take it, have denied that force had its place in the enforcement of law, and that it must often be used to make law effective. Yet he would not admit that you could build law on the use of force to the exclusion of everything else, as he supposed Holmes did, an anti-Christian idea that seemed to dismiss morals from law, and narrow it to brute force. But Justice Holmes's observation about force was a description of what he saw happen. It was not an attempt to exhaust the definition of law or to reduce it to a single formula. No one who had read *The Common Law* with understanding, or studied Holmes's contribution to law over half a century, could possibly have made the foolish mistake of believing that Holmes meant to banish other conceptions of law by this particular criterion. To him law involved many other attributes—it was an expression of life, the formulation of community desires, the act of a legislature or the decree of a sovereign, the intuition or prejudice of a judge written into an opinion; but—and he thought it vitally important to keep repeating the idea in the striking form of an oversimplification—all law rested on the exercise of force for its fulfillment.

Father Ford, trembling a little as he tries to hold his spear in place, takes the next step: if law is based on force no law can be absolute, and what Holmes called rights are not fundamental or eternal, since they rest on the ephemeral and temporary quality of force.

By definition Holmes uses the word *right* in the narrow legal sense as something that can be enforced, not in the secondary and more ambiguous meaning of a desirable end, such as the pursuit of happiness, an activity to which men may believe they are entitled but which cannot be achieved through a court of law.

The children at Little Rock did not enjoy their right to go to a public school until United States troops saw to it that the right was enforced. When by statute the Nazi regime destroyed the right of the German-Jewish population to live where they pleased, to own their own property, to come and go freely, to marry Gentiles—in a word to enjoy the common decencies of tolerance and equality of living won for human beings over the long centuries—Jews no longer enjoyed *rights* in the Holmesian sense. That they existed undiminished in Father Ford's head (or heart), or in that distant

Heaven where Jews take their place with Christians and Moham-medans, since natural law is universal; or in the mind of God, since natural law came from Him—assuming all these subjective abso-lutes of religion, which may be peculiarly important to those who have been deprived of the enforcement of their legal rights on earth, can it be doubted that Father Ford would have admitted that there is such a thing as an enforceable legal right? And the Justice would have answered that that was all he meant; and that those were the only kind of rights he was talking about. His own views were "simple and brutal" when he considered *legal* rights.

But Holmes knew that even though a sovereign does create legal rights, and makes you obey them, he is often hopelessly wrong morally. Holmes did not dismiss human aspirations, and re-membered that they embodied principles that men had died for, and that it was well not to forget, the "right"—particularly for him—to think and talk freely. He believed in the articulation of these rights, but was not prepared to say that they were eternal. He lamented the tendency "toward underrating or forgetting the safeguards in bills of rights that had to be fought for in their day and that still are worth fighting for." What he understood by human rights was what a given crowd would fight for suc-cessfully. Old Louis Agassiz, he remembered, once said that in some part of Germany if you added a farthing to the price of a glass of beer there would be a revolution. If that was true, to have beer at the current price was one of the rights of man in that place.

Father Ford can have his absolute law, Holmes would say, if he keeps within his jurisdiction, the imagination of the faithful, and does not trespass on Caesar's sterner magistracy, where courts ap-ply the rules that govern men. And that is what Holmes said in a dozen different ways, some of which Father Ford finds pretty hard to understand, as indeed they are.

Holmes's tight condensations—there is hardly ever an extra word to ease the understanding—do not tend to clarify his basic meaning. He liked to say that he wrote for the one man who did understand—but sometimes Holmes missed him.

FATHER FORD bravely tackles the Justice's famous statement in his article on *Natural Law*, which has proved the target for so many shafts: "But for legal purposes a right is only the hypostasis of a prophecy—the imagination of a substance supporting the fact that the public force will be brought to bear upon those who do things said to contravene it—just as we talk of the force of gravitation accounting for the conduct of bodies in space." Even Sir Frederick balked a bit at this—the word "hypostasis" was known to him only as a theological term—in what sense did Holmes use it? To start his definition of law, Holmes replied, he employed the word in the sense in which it is used by the modern lawyer, as a statement of the circumstances in which the public force would be brought to bear upon men through the courts: that is the prophecy in general terms. "So we prophesy that the earth and sun will act towards each other in a certain way. Then we pretend to account for that mode of action by the hypothetical cause, the force of gravitation, which is merely the hypostasis of the prophesied fact and an empty phrase. So we get up the empty substratum, a *right*, to pretend to account for the fact that the courts will act in a certain way." And this applied even to a right which Father Ford regards as absolute and God-given. Holmes added, almost as if he were trying to be doubly offensive: "I think our morally tinted words have caused a great deal of confused thinking." But Father Ford makes no comment, after quoting this passage, but merely adds that Pollock agreed with Holmes about *right*, an ambiguous word meaning an expectation that the court would assist you, in case of interference with certain of your *lawful* liberties, or that you could call on the court for redress of some form. Apparently Sir Frederick was highly respectable company!

What did *morally tinted* mean? Father Ford, pondering, and putting all these assertions together, concluded that Holmes divorced the ethical from the legal order. That is an accurate reflection; but the priest went on to add that Holmes denied *any* relation between law and morals. Apparently Father Ford had either not read Holmes or not understood what he was talking about. The Justice invariably assumed the relationship of morals and law, insisting, as I have noted, that the prevalent moral and political theories have had their part in determining the rules whereby men are governed. He did not wish his hearers to misinterpret what he had to say about force as the language of cynicism: "The law is the witness and the external deposit of our moral life. Its history is the history of the moral development of the race."

AS A LAWYER, Holmes used the word "theories"; Father Ford, a priest, spoke of "principles." Holmes, unlike Father Ford, never experienced an absolute. He called his preferences "prejudices" because as an historian he realized how the "prejudices which judges share with their fellow-men" had shaped the rules of law, and he had watched those of some of the other justices on the Court on which he sat prevent them from upholding laws which interfered with the dogma of laissez faire which they held sacred. Father Ford should have known what Holmes meant by *morally tinted,* for he quotes at length from Holmes's wonderful address, "The Path of the Law," at the dedication of a new hall of the Boston University School of Law in 1897.

If you want to know the law, and nothing else, Holmes had said, you must look only for its material consequences, which you can predict, like a "bad man," who cares only for results, not like a good one, who finds his reasons for conduct "in the vaguer sanctions of his conscience." The law is full of phraseology drawn from morals, and talks about *rights* and *duties, malice, intent,* and *negligence*—and nothing is easier in legal reasoning than to take these words in their moral sense. So we speak of the rights of a man meaning to mark the limits of interference with individual freedom prescribed by conscience, or by our ideal. Yet many laws have been passed and enforced which go beyond the limit of interference, and are condemned by the most enlightened public opinion. Therefore nothing but confusion can result from assuming that the rights of man in a moral sense are equally rights in the sense of the Constitution and the law.

If the training of lawyers, Holmes believed, led them habitually to consider more definitely and explicitly the social advantages on which the rule they lay down must be justified, they sometimes would hesitate where now they are confident, and see that really they were taking sides upon debatable and often burning questions. And judges—"There is a tendency to think of judges," Holmes wrote Laski in 1926, "as if they were independent mouthpieces of the infinite, and not simply directors of a force that comes from the source that gives them their authority. I think our court has fallen into the error at times and it is that that I have aimed at when I have said that the Common Law is not a brooding omnipresence in the sky and that the U.S. is not subject to some mystic overlaw that it is bound to obey." To Holmes there was no such thing as *the* common law *in abstracto*.

And that is precisely how he thought of natural law—a mystic overlaw, not law in any true sense, theology or morals if you like, but not law. The demand for the superlative that we find in all men was at the bottom of the philosopher's effort to prove that truth was absolute, and of the jurist's search for criteria of universal validity which he collects under the head of natural law. That is why the jurists who believed in natural law seemed to him to be "in that naive state of mind that accepts what has been familiar and accepted by them and their neighbors as something that must be accepted by all men everywhere." To a Jesuit priest, reared on natural law, Holmes's view that it was but a product of wishful thinking must have sounded blasphemous.

THE UNDERLYING DIFFERENCE between the views of Justice Holmes and the Jesuits boils down to whether or not you believe in absolutes; or, more accurately put, whether you think they have an existence of their own, outside the mind of man. Apparently natural law, for instance, in addition to existing in the mind of the Creator, and in the mind of man when he exercised his reason in order to find it, was conceived as something with a separate being of its own, irrespective of divine or human recognition. Holmes had never experienced it, and, not believing in revelations which he had not shared, denied its external validity. The unwillingness to accept less than being on the ground floor with God did not impress him much except as a fact of psychology. The assumption of a knowledge of ultimate truth implied a kind of arrogance that he distrusted. Why should we not be humble? Why not admit that the first primordial wiggle came before our time?

By no means a humble man himself, Holmes experienced humility when he thought of the universe, of which he was so minute a part. His comments were most caustic when he was dealing with those who were sure that they had universal truth by the ears. "I think the proper attitude," he wrote to Pollock, "is that we know nothing of cosmic values and bow our heads—seeing reason enough for doing all we can and not demanding the plan of campaign of the

General. . . . It's enough for me that this universe can produce intelligence and ideals." He could not go along, he said in another letter, with "some mystical works of men seeking to lift themselves by the slack of their own breeches, and demanding that the final compulsions under which we reason, love, etc., should be admitted as of cosmic validity. I stop short of that. All I mean by truth is the road I can't help travelling. What the worth of that *can't help* may be I have no means of knowing. Perhaps the universe, if there is one, has no truth outside the finiteness of man." This position is not an extreme one. It does not exclude another's experience of faith, but implies it is not his—Holmes knows his own, but would not force it on anyone else.

He thought clericism childish, and at times was a little disturbed at exhibitions of ecclesiastic power. But he had such a conviction that it was doomed that he did not care to hurry its fate; and, ad interim, it helped to keep order. He also questioned the postulate of science that everything can be explained. He had a sense of the mystery of the universe, and thought it unlikely that we know anything about it or have faculties that fit us to do more than adjust ourselves to it and to live. He had faith in the prevalence of reason, but was aware how long reason may be kept under by what man wants to believe.

Such a point of view, it may be conceded, would not be popular among believers in the reality of eternal truth.

But all this is in the realm of speculation. The issue raised by the detractors of Holmes is sharper and more immediate than any found in the play of moral theorizing. Holmes never went out of his way to discuss natural law, except for the casual reference that I have described; or indeed, any other religion—systems, whether religious or philosophic, bored him. He had no particular objection to indulgence in their intricacies if they did not impinge on his own field of law. He did not agree with what Edmund Burke, whom he liked to quote, had said about law—that it sharpened the mind only to narrow it. To Holmes law was the reflection of man's life on earth; and, more particularly, the story of the experience of his own people, and was therefore worthy of the devotion of a lifetime. He had discovered that law was not the same as morals, which differed from creed to creed, and that it was highly dangerous to try to preserve it in the form of a moral absolute—for life kept changing and absolutes did not. He had seen men clothe their predilections in the generalities of ideals that had become standardized, and close their minds to an appropriate solution of the practical problem of decision that was before them.

THAT NATURAL LAW is taught in Roman Catholic law schools as part of the education of a lawyer deflects him from the modern approach to law as a science, dragging theology back into law from which, as in the teaching of medicine and other professions, it had long since been banished, except in the Catholic schools. Only Catholic law schools teach that natural law has a higher and more august sanction than human law; that laws in contravention of natural law are invalid; and that any statute or decision conflicting with natural law is inherently vitiated. In other schools "law" is not taught as being eternal, and could not be, for the modern lawyer, pragmatic and scientific as far as possible in his approach, has learned to keep his law and religion apart. It is to this separation that the Catholic teachers object.

The Catholic doctrine—fundamentally inconsistent with separation of Church and State—goes much further than the concept that, in determining whether he should resist a particular law thought to be evil a man should bide by the dictates of his conscience, since it insists that he must obey the dictates of his Church, irrespective of the expressed will of his sovereign. To the Catholic, natural law is what the Church says it is.

This potential conflict is, however, more startling in theory than in practice, for a theorem of the Church holds that although the basic tenets of natural law never change, their application varies. Thus right to a fair trial is said to be basic, unchangeable, a law of God and of nature; but a particular application of this general right, such as the right to trial by a jury, is not a natural law right, and therefore not absolute, and may be given or withdrawn by the State. One is eternal, the other temporary. Since questions of law arise on specific issues, and not over the discussion of principles, there is in practice little conflict between natural law and the law of the sovereign.

But the effect of such a doctrine on the development of law is important. Even if now for practical purposes there is little conflict—although for hundreds of years the struggle for temporal power between Church and State was savage and continuous—the suggestion that there is a higher lawgiving power than the State postulates the theological approach. This way of looking at law is against everything that Holmes stood for.

FATHER LUCEY, coming back to the attack, in an article which he called "Holmes—Liberal—Humanitarian—Believer in Democracy?" admitted that once upon a time he had been charmed by the Justice's style and the "end results of his opinions involving personal liberties," but later had an uneasy feeling that there was something wrong with his idol. For the next few years he read and reread everything that Holmes had written. And what did he find? "A philosophical skeleton of life and law, of man and morals that was horribly deformed."

This language, like Father Kenealy's, partakes of the rhetorical; but in spite of its ineptness we do get a sense that Father Lucey was upset. He insisted that skepticism, pragmatism, and evolution were the influences which inevitably led to Holmes's position. Holmes would not have liked to be called a pragmatist, for the word indicated a philosophy which he thought ridiculous, so that when Laski spoke of "the implicit pragmatism" of Holmes's attitude, the Justice answered that *the judging of law by its efforts and results* did not have to wait for William James or Roscoe Pound for its existence.

But skepticism and pragmatism were characteristic of the age in which the father had been reared, and against which his Church, knowing the disastrous fashion in which indulgence in such heresies endangered her own authority, had continually thundered. Therefore to find these influences displayed by still another great man could hardly account for the father's choler. I suspect that what really shocked the priest was Holmes's language rather than his views. As the old song goes, It wasn't so much as what he said as the orful way he said it! Father Lucey may have remembered, although he did not quote it, what Holmes said about the martyr —that he was *a pigheaded adherent of an inadequate idea.*

Holmes opened himself widely to criticism. In spite of the fact that he distrusted sweeping statements, and all his life resisted their pressure, he could, for the sake of a telling *bon mot* or neat aphorism, let out the most absurd generalities, worded as if they were self-evident truths, as when he said to Laski that "all law means I will kill you if necessary to make you conform to my requirements." Sometimes he goes on to explain what he means— law, he adds here, is what the sovereign orders: "If in fact Catholics or atheists are proscribed and the screws put on, it seems to me idle to say that it is not law because by a theory that you and I hold . . . it ought not to be." He keeps coming back to the idea that men either agreed or fought: "When men differ in taste as to the kind of world they want the only thing to do is to go to work killing."

It was all right if you did not take Holmes literally, did not go along with the inclusive sweep of his oversimplifications. His theory that law was nothing more than the prophecy of what the judge would hold, was useful for the counseling lawyer—for the solicitor—but not for the trial lawyer bent on persuading the court, the barrister: law is of course something more than prophecy.

In his article on natural law Holmes remarked that he used to say, when he was young, *that truth was the majority vote of that nation that could lick all others.* Father Lucey comments eloquently: "This of course was Hitler's test . . . the theme song of the Storm Troops as they made their pragmatic functional approach to Poland, Czechoslovakia, Norway, Holland, Belgium, and France." But the father did not mention that Holmes went on to explain the sense in which he had made the remark: "Certainly we may expect that the received opinion about the present war [the First World War] will depend a good deal upon which side wins (I hope with all my soul it will be mine), and I think that the statement was correct in so far as it implied that our test of truth is a reference to either a present or an imagined future majority in favor of our view." This was not unlike Mr. Dooley's line about the Supreme Court's following the elections—neither was the whole truth and nothing but the truth, but each had a core of meaning.

Holmes had written Pollock that when one thinks coldly he could see no reason for attributing to man a significance different *in kind* (he did not say in degree) from that which belongs to a baboon or to a grain of sand. Father Lucey seized on the phrase but lost its point: "Stripped of a soul and innate dignity," he lamented, "man is only as significant as a baboon or grain of sand." What Holmes meant was that since the universe was without guidance, there was no one to assert differences or draw comparisons. Holmes would not have admitted that there was no difference between himself and Father Lucey, or between Father Lucey and a baboon. He meant only that, cosmically speaking, the universe did not make the distinction. Father Lucey, one would have thought, would have hesitated to speak about what went on inside the complex and subtle mind which he called Holmes's world, and to say that for Holmes there were no values inside the law or outside it. Holmes's values were as precious to him as Father Lucey's; but no man as dogmatic as Father Lucey could ever admit that a freethinker could have a creed that was noble.

Twenty years later Holmes wrote along similar lines to Pollock that a platitude had come home to him with quasi-religious force. He had been repining at the thought of his slow progress—how few ideas he had or had picked up—when it occurred to him to think of the total of life, and how the greater part was wholly absorbed in living and continuing life—victuals, procreation, rest, and eternal terror. Why not accept the common lot? An adequate vitality would say: "God—what a good sleep I've had." "My eye, that was a dinner." "Now for a rattling walk." Functioning is all there is—only, our keenest pleasure is what we call the higher sort. "I wonder," he finished, "if cosmically an idea is any more important than the bowels." The bowels! No wonder Father Lucey called Holmes "an animal man"—a designation which would have mightily pleased our Judge—and added that Holmes's concept of democracy embodied "a strong jungle odor."

One accusation Father Lucey made that might have angered Holmes—a patently unfair charge—was that if "the law on the books clashed with Holmes's evolutionary theory Holmes could stretch the law and try to work off his theory." Holmes spent his life keeping his own preferences and theories out of his opinions. It was a small and mean observation, and Father Lucey made no attempt to support it by citing any decision. Now and then the father becomes personal, sneering that Holmes spent his spare time with youngsters "whom he felt were the smart minds of their generation and the elite of the future." The priest must have had some individuals in mind, although he does not name them—

Owen Wister, Justice Frankfurter, Walter Lippmann, Lord Eustace Percy?—they came to be numbered among the elite. Finally Father Lucey whips himself into a mild canonical frenzy, pelting "the Yankee from Olympus" (to use the father's words) with soft absolutes—*skepticism, evolutionism, positivism, and pragmatism*—that reduce men to "a pestilence-driven multitude, the prey of a blind evolutionary climate!"

This is no inconsequential battle, he cries, not only for Americans, but for the entire world. If universal agnosticism prevail it will mean the end of Democracy, because there can be no Democracy without protection of absolute natural rights. . . . Holmesian philosophy was infiltrating the public schools. Had not J. Edgar Hoover testified before the Kefauver Committee that we are in a moral depression, and added, as one of the reasons, that the name of God could not be mentioned in many of our schools? The Holmesian philosophy had reached the very summit—we find "the Chief Justice of the United States [Fred M. Vinson] proclaiming in an official document [Father Lucey means an opinion]: *Nothing is more certain in modern society than the principle that there are no absolutes . . . all concepts are relative.*" But the father does not believe that the Chief Justice really realized the implications to which he was committing himself.

AT TIMES Father Lucey seems to be angry with what eludes him. But the difference between the two men is not principally a question of misunderstanding. It comes down to a determination of the *sources* of general principles. The Catholics say that they come from God, and have a validity entirely independent of their human acceptance. For Justice Holmes they are derived from the consensus of the community embodied in the long tradition of the law, of the dominant beliefs of the culture of which he felt himself a part, and of the Constitutional provisions expressing that culture.

Put simply, and without the paradoxes and teasing oversimplifications, Holmes's beliefs are neither radical—for our day and age—nor disturbing: the belief that men make their own laws; that these laws do not flow from some mysterious omnipresence in the sky, and that judges are not independent mouthpieces of the infinite; that since morality is human in its origin and its end, men should be permitted to discover what is for them desirable and how it should be achieved, and allowed to indulge in their own legislative experiments to better their lot—they are not fools for doing what they want to do; that the justification of any rule of law is that it helps to bring about a desired social end; that law must change to follow the needs of man; that all doctrine must be adjusted to these needs; that the law when ascertained should be obeyed, but will not be ascertained by reference to vague generalities, or by fumbling over the familiar; and finally that we cannot think beyond the reach in time of our own society, so that the claim of a special code to respect is not that it represents first principles but simply that it exists and is the one to which we have become accustomed.

THERE CAN NEVER BE reconciliation between the dogmatic mind and the free mind. In spite of efforts to bridge the gap between those who cherish some Being outside their own world because they cannot bear the terror of standing alone, and men like Holmes who find their strength and faith within themselves, the chasm remains, and it is idle to deny its depth. The fanatic believer, who cannot view those who do not agree with him except as evil men, must never be tolerant, for tolerance might open the gates of understanding.

III

THE SUPREME COURT

An Approach to Decisions

IN MY LAST LECTURE I DISCUSSED

Holmes's view of natural law and similar moral absolutes and the
resulting attacks on this outlook in law journals, chiefly by Jesuit
priests.

I shall now inquire what standards if any should be relied on
by judges in approaching difficult questions of constitutional interpretation. Is there any fundamental principle or set of principles
that should be born in mind, that suggest the direction, that create
the appropriate basis for judgment? Can judges be helped by ethical points of view, by the tenets of natural law, or by the reaches of
any other general standards? And if there is a guide, can it be defined in general terms that can be applied to specific cases? Justice
Holmes distrusted generalities; but of necessity he had to resort to
them in formulating an approach to his work.

In September, 1955, this problem was discussed at a conference in celebration of the two hundredth anniversary of the birth of Chief Justice Marshall, assembled at the Harvard Law School to consider the ideal of government under law—an ideal which, as Erwin N. Griswold, Dean of the Law School, pointed out, gave rise to great difficulties both in theory and practice in its application to the daily business of government. It was recognized that the function of the courts in practice had a substantial legislative aspect, and an effort was made by many of the speakers to find some rationale which would be useful to judges in choosing between opposing convictions, each claimed to be supported by some principle found in the Constitution or the law.

It was a representative group, which included Professor André Tune of the University of Grenoble, who had written extensively about the constitutional system in the United States; Baron Evershed of Stapenhill, Master of the Rolls since 1949; Sir Owen Dixon, Chief Justice of Australia, who underscored Chief Justice Marshall's influence on the making of the Australian constitution; and the Honorable Albert Van de Sandt Centlivres, Chief Justice of South Africa. There were distinguished American lawyers and judges who joined in the discussions, among them the Chief Justice of the Supreme Court of the United States, and Justice Frankfurter; Judge William H. Hastie of the Court of Appeals of the Third Circuit, and Judge Charles E. Wyzanski, Jr., of the United States District Court of Massachusetts; John Lord O'Brian, an outstanding leader of the American bar; and Professor Herbert Wechsler of the Columbia Law School, with his broad background of public service, teaching, and writing.

The discussion ranged over many aspects of law and government. There were not, it seemed to me when I read the addresses and comments,* many sharp expressions of difference in approach; and too much eagerness for agreement, particularly in the com-

* They are collected in *Government Under Law,* Harvard University Press, 1956.

ments which came after each talk, perhaps accounted for by the anxiety of everyone to see and follow some beckoning light, some vision above the clash of strongly felt views, added to the American assumption that it was not quite good manners to disagree, deferentially accepted by their distinguished guests.

One had a sense that the speakers were groping for something new—an age was behind them, an era past: neither Darwin nor Einstein nor Freud nor William James was now enough. I found little evidence of a desire to turn back to the theological security of the eighteenth century, or to abandon the scientific (and skeptical) approach on which Holmes insisted, and which he believed was necessary for a mature realization of the place of law in life. The search for general assumptions that underlay law was not impeded by the frequent assertion that all things changed, for, with few exceptions, the participants assumed or emphasized the fact that these principles cannot be absolute, and must be reviewed, however slowly, as the circumstances to which they were once applicable altered or disappeared.

John Lord O'Brian laid stress on the change rather than on the endurance, yet insisted that the time-honored values did endure. He spoke of the new interpretation of the Constitution deliberately adopted by the United States Supreme Court to meet the new conditions that had arisen early in this century. The broader interpretation had been noticeable in the last twenty years in the so-called New Deal Court, and involved particularly an alteration in the conception of due process, which is no longer used to block the passage of social legislation. Formerly the guarantee of due process was interpreted to sustain the liberty of the employer to contract as he pleased; now it is conceived to justify a statute which confers rights that are fundamental to the liberty of the employee, and interference with them is thought a proper subject for legislative condemnation, as the Court said in the *Jones & Laughlin* case.

Yet one cannot separate economic and social considerations from political and moral tenets with which they are almost invariably entangled. If changes in the application of the Bill of Rights and of due process do occur, the implications behind them have also altered to meet new economic needs. Chancellor Kent sensed the dilemma, but was not troubled by it. He first made himself "master of the facts," he wrote, and then "sat down to search the authorities." He "almost always found principles suited to his view of the case."

Father Joseph M. Snee, S.J., Professor of Law at Georgetown University, had no difficulty with this ancient quandary of permanence in the midst of change, since, confessing himself a "medievalist," he found in the reaches of natural law the eternal values which are the basis of all man-made law, and which cannot change. Their application, not their essence, varies from time to time, as new circumstances arise, but natural-law rights endure forever. Father Snee believed that the gradual erosion of liberty in our generation had made us skeptical of the very skepticism which denied any philosophic foundation for man's freedom. He defined the rights that must be protected in any free society in the Supreme Court's language: "individual rights to life, liberty, and property"; "a fundamental principle of liberty and justice which inheres in the very idea of free government"; freedoms which are "implicit in the concept of ordered liberty"; "canons of decency and fairness"; "considerations deeply rooted in reason and in the compelling traditions of the legal profession."

All of these impeccable expressions have the high vague ring of natural law about them. Can you think of a lawyer—or a layman —who would quarrel with such unexceptional assertions? But can remembrance of the sound of their language guide a judge in deciding whether a government employee, believed to be of Communist persuasion, should be discharged from employment by his government without being allowed to confront the witness who, perhaps on neighborly gossip, charged him? Here two fundamen-

tal principles clash, about which reasonable men differ earnestly
—protection of the state from subversion and preservation of the
right of an accused man to confront his accusers. Such admirable
phrases, however, do not help a judge to make a specific decision,
and are too often employed to implement the ultimately personal
choice in the particular case, and clothe the opinion with the appearance of moral necessity.

Yet because we must agree that general principles alter over a
period of time, and that they cannot solve specific issues, it should
be casually concluded that they have no place in government under
law. Once we admit that they are not eternal, the dilemma disap-
pears, and we can recognize their value within that period of time
when they are still accepted as expressing the point of view of the
community. This was what Justice Holmes meant when in the
first opinion that he delivered for the Supreme Court of the United
States, he spoke of a constitution *embodying only relatively fundamental rules of right, as generally understood by all English-speak-
ing communities*. If these rules are understood to be relatively
fundamental, and not to be thought of as eternal principles, they
are less apt to become the *partisan of a particular set of ethical or
economical opinions*. Claims to everlasting truth are apt to smack
of the partisan approach.

JUDGE WYZANSKI, in his address to the
conference, realized the limitation of general constitutional doctrines much as Holmes had thought of them, and could find no
corpus of principles derived from natural law or from any other
theory of social justice which would help judges settle the major
questions of foreign affairs, of the rates of taxation, of the objects
of expenditure, of the regulation of enterprise, or of due process

by government. But even if constitutionalism cannot be defined or maintained by reference to abstractions, the judges, by deciding concrete cases, mold the people's view of durable principles of government, and create an awareness of basic issues concretely illustrated in courts—and, Judge Wyzanski adds—constitutionalism may be built on a system of immaterial values that make men believe they are masters of the State. In the United States the Constitution reminds us of our whole history, a history which helps us govern ourselves. Popular education and popular habits play a vital part in maintaining the standards of society. This is not a fiction, but the respect we must pay to the myths on which the people have their being.

In Judge Wyzanski's view courts are there to decide specific issues and not to apply eternal principles to stubborn difficulties. The absolutes have their place, and their value cannot be ignored. Relatively thought of, they have an importance that Judge Wyzanski and other speakers recognized. Established over a long period of time, they have acquired a broad area of acceptance by the community and have come to be clothed with the appearance of eternal truth. Precisely because they can be simply stated and have been rendered uncontroversial over the years of long general agreement, they are stated and restated in Supreme Court decisions at the same time that their application is in dispute. We tend to forget how much the acceptance of these principles by the courts and by the public goes to preserve what we stand for, as Holmes would have been the first to admit. They grow indirectly from a collection of many instances, over the years, and evolve as the facts change. In a settled society like ours the change is slow, and after a time we do not remember that the principle, or more accurately stated the practice, has changed, and look back on our ancestors as quaint or cruel because we have learned to think differently. No one today in America or England would urge that torture was justified to elicit a confession of guilt, although, only a few hundred years ago, its use was generally approved.

JUDGE WYZANSKI SAID that principles of natural law did not help judges settle major questions. But every now and then natural law creeps into a Supreme Court opinion. A comparatively recent decision, *Adamson v. California,* contained a reference to natural law that drew a lively attack from three dissenting justices, voiced by Justice Black. Under a California law, which permitted him to do so, a state prosecutor commented on the defendant's failure to take the stand, and he was convicted. The Court assumed that if this had occurred in a Federal court the Fifth Amendment, which outlaws self-incrimination, would have been violated, irrespective of the act of Congress that forbids such comment. For some time before the *Adamson* case the Court had held that certain "fundamental" provisions of the Bill of Rights (but not all) applied to state courts under the provision of the Fourteenth Amendment calling for due process. Was this particular procedural protection of a defendant—to be shielded from comment if he did not testify—such a basic right that it must not be infringed by state law?

The California Supreme Court sustained the conviction, a judgment which the United States Supreme Court upheld.

Justice Reed wrote the majority opinion, holding that the question had already been settled by former decisions. Justice Frankfurter felt impelled to file a concurring opinion, and Justice Black to attack it. Frankfurter insisted that the "right" in question was not an "ultimate decency in a civilized society," and (in Cardozo's words in a previous decision) "essential to a fair and enlightened system of justice"; nor was its denial inconsistent with the practices of a truly free society. He added that in the history of thought natural law has had a much longer and much better founded meaning and justification than such "suggestive selection of the first eight Amendments for incorporation into the Fourteenth."

Such reliance on natural law against the Bill of Rights—as it appeared to him—was bound to rouse Justice Black, who in a dissent expressed his belief that it gave the Court power to expand and contract constitutional standards to conform to its conception of what at a particular time constitutes civilized decency; and acceptance of the "natural-law-due-process formula degrades constitutional safeguards"—the Court should not be permitted to "roam at large in the broad expanses of policy and morals." Father Snee would probably have considered that this was an example of what he had meant by the application of natural law differing from its ultimate principle—a man must have a fair trial, but it could be had without excluding comment on his failure to testify; and this is precisely what Reed held: that there was no violation of a right to a fair trial.

A later case, *Rochin v. California,* involved the same clash between points of view. The facts were unusual. Two police officers raided the house of a suspected possessor of narcotics. When asked about two pills on a table next his bed he hastily swallowed them. He was taken to a hospital, his stomach pumped out, the pills, containing morphine, came up, and on this evidence he was convicted. The Court reversed. Frankfurter, writing for the whole Court, suggested that the "vague contours of due process" did not leave the judges at large, and talked about "considerations deeply rooted in reason and in the compelling traditions of the legal profession." He took pains to add, as if to correct any misapprehension of what he had said in the *Adamson* case: "Due process of law thus conceived is not to be derided as a resort to a revival of natural law." He introduced another standard, more complex, but hardly more useful in practice than those which had preceded it, addressed to the qualities society has a right to expect from judges: "an evaluation based on a disinterested inquiry pursued in the spirit of science, on a balanced order of facts exactly and fairly stated, on the detached consideration of conflicting claims . . . —not *ad hoc* and episodic but duly mindful of reconciling the needs both of continuity and of change."

But the *ad hoc* approach surely colored and perhaps decided both cases. In the *Adamson* case the comment by the prosecutor did not shock a majority of the judges; but in the *Rochin* the use of a stomach pump shocked everyone! Both Black and Douglas, although concurring in the decision, expressed their disagreement with Frankfurter's approach: "Nebulous standards," said Black; and Douglas pointed out that nine state courts—a majority of those deciding the question—would have admitted the evidence, so there was no use talking about the "decencies of civilized conduct." The rule must be formulated by the justices themselves.

BUT TO RETURN to the Marshall conference. Professor Wechsler, commenting on Father Snee's discussion, put his finger on a point worth remembering. Our Constitution must be suited to a varied people and should draw strength not from a single philosophic system but from the total system of ideas; and we must assume that we are "united in belief in norms of right and justice that transcend positive law, yielding criteria—broad as they are—by which all government and law may properly be judged." A wise observation—but are we any further along? Those norms do not suggest a criterion for deciding the case of our alleged Comumnist friend. Wechsler shrewdly added that the Court's function of declaring laws unconstitutional presents essentially political problems. We are nearer understanding our difficulty—whether the suspectedly subversive employee can be fired without a safeguard commonly afforded in a trial is a political (in a broad sense) rather than a moral question: or, to put it in a more persuasive light, whether the issue should be dealt with on the political level, where compromise is more easily arrived at, than on a moral plateau with its clash of perhaps exemplary but usually irreconcilable predilections.

Outlining his approach a little further, Wechsler suggested that the judicial power should be exercised with moderation, and that it is abidingly supported as an instrument of sober second thought by the political branches of our government which it sometimes checks. Very well put; but it must be remembered that only yesterday (and doubtless tomorrow) those branches have been breathing hotly on the necks of the exalted brethren and will continue to do so—not always a healthy check by democratically elected power on undemocratically appointed authority. Caution, neutrality, and generality of formulation, "however uncongenial to the factionalists"—these are Wechsler's norms; and he adds the comforting thought that courts rarely interpose a final bar to legislation.

MR. JUSTICE FRANKFURTER, delivering, as might have been expected, one of the most thoughtful contributions to the discussion, was sure that Marshall thought of law—as did Holmes—as legally enforceable rights; and that when Marshall used the phrase "natural law" it was not much more than "literary garniture," and not a guiding means of adjudication. Natural law, he continued, as Sir Frederick Pollock had written Holmes, was regarded in the Middle Ages as the senior branch of divine law and therefore had to be treated as infallible; but, Pollock added, "there was no infallible way of knowing what it was." Frankfurter, who has followed the Holmes tradition on the Supreme Court, reminded his audience that the vast developing present-day role of law was not the design of a statesman nor was it attributable to the influence of some great thinker—or, he might have added, of revelation: it was the reflection of the technological revolution, and had become an essential accompaniment of the shift to the service state—the same change for which Mr. O'Brian had found it difficult to offer a satisfactory explanation.

The fact that judicial review is a deliberate check upon democracy through an organ of government not subject to popular control adds to the duty of the justices not to act on merely personal views. For those who exercise this extraordinary authority, a breadth of outlook is demanded, and an invincible disinterestedness rooted in temperament and confirmed by discipline. Such vague constitutional provisions as due process and equal protection of the laws, he insisted, quoting Judge Learned Hand, "represent a mood rather than a command," and catch color from changing times. He did not say that there are no enduring standards in the light of which the judiciary may enforce constitutional provisions, but hinted in that direction by recommending a "sturdy doubt" that one had found them.

By reminding us of the limitations of the judicial role; of its humane and gradualist tradition; of the pervasiveness throughout the whole range of government of the spirit of law, and its endeavors of reason; of how the standards of what is fair and just set by courts promote the spirit of law throughout government; by emphasizing all these values Justice Frankfurter has suggested the mood of an approach that courts have taken and should take. He admits, at the same time, that he has not been able to "fashion criteria for easier adjudication of the specific cases." Is that perhaps as far as we can go in trying to discover what principles should guide a judge in solving a specific problem? Must principles be reduced to a mood, cautious by tradition, tolerant, turning for help chiefly to Holmes's felt necessities of the time, and the prevalent moral and political theories and intuitions of public policy?

LIKE HOLMES, Frankfurter distrusts not only abstractions to solve issues but also phrases to implement their validity. As an example he cites the famous expression of Justice Holmes, "clear and present danger," to describe the limit when speech should no longer be considered protected by the First Amendment.

The "clear and present danger" guide, so often repeated, first appeared in the *Schenck* case, one of a series of three sedition cases arising out of the First World War, which Chief Justice White had assigned to Holmes, knowing his preference for uncurbed talk. In all three, Holmes sustained convictions under the Espionage Act; and in the *Debs* case affirmed a conviction for obstructing the recruiting service of the United States in speeches opposing the war. Two weeks after the decisions had been delivered, Holmes, evidently troubled, sent copies of them to Harold Laski, saying that he "greatly regretted having to write them—and (*between ourselves*) that the Government had pressed them to a hearing." He knew that "donkeys and knaves" would represent the Court as concurring in the condemnation of Debs—who had been the candidate of the Socialists for President four times—because he was a dangerous agitator. Of course, Holmes added, so far as he was concerned, Debs might "split his guts" without Holmes interfering with him, or sanctioning interference. Agitators bored Holmes, but he disliked bottling them up. He had no doubt about the law—the First Amendment did not protect Debs. The Federal judges seemed to him to have gotten hysterical about the war, and he thought the President (Woodrow Wilson, who was at the time preaching acceptance of the League of Nations across the country) "when he gets through his present amusements might do some pardoning." Three weeks later Holmes told Pollock that he was beginning to get stupid letters of protest against the decision that Debs was rightly convicted of obstructing the recruiting service, *so far as the law was concerned.* "There was a lot of jaw about free speech," which he had dealt with "somewhat summarily," in the *Schenck* case. He added, a little wistfully, that, as it happened, he would go further than the majority in favor of free speech, and it was partly on that account that the C.J. had assigned the cases to him.

The *New Republic* had been critical of the decision in the *Debs* case, and Holmes wrote the editor, Herbert Croly, that since in the *Schenck* case the constitutionality of the Espionage Act had been sustained, all that he had to do in the *Debs* case was to refer to that decision. "I hated," he said, "to write the *Debs* case, and still more those of the other poor devils before us the same day and the week before." He thought that if he had been on the jury he would have been for acquittal. But the clauses under consideration not only were constitutional but were *proper enough while the war was on.* When people are putting out all their energies in battle, it was not unreasonable to say we won't have obstacles intentionally put in the way of raising troops—by persuasion any more than by force.

These cases illustrate Holmes's characteristic approach to decisions. He made it very plain where his sympathies lay. He commented to Pollock that the defendants seemed to him "poor fools whom I should have been inclined to pass over if I could"—but he did not permit his inclinations to overcome his judgment. There could be no question that Congress had the right to punish obstructions of the draft, particularly during a war. If speech was intentionally designed to produce immediately the substantive evil prohibited by the statute—a question for the jury—the verdict must be sustained.

LET US FOR a moment return to our hypothetical case, and speculate on how Holmes would have determined the issue. I have suggested that the application of general principles, which may be useful in disposing of "easy" cases, where there is substantially no disagreement, does not help us in solving the "tough" issues, in which important public policies conflict—in this instance due process against the importance of protecting the government from internal disloyalty.

To sharpen the issue I shall be more specific on the facts. I assume that the question arises under a Federal statute specifically authorizing the dismissal of a government employee for being a member of an organization advocating the overthrow of the United States Government by force or violence, and approving the use of a procedure which permits the government to rely on secret evidence, without confronting the employee with the witness.

I suggest that Holmes—a first-rate legal craftsman—would have tackled the problem by first taking a look at the Constitution. He would have examined the history of the due process clause—which the defendant was invoking—and the conditions from which it emerged and which gave it content. He would have sought to find its purpose and meaning, and the legal tradition behind it. He would have noted that the Constitution provided for confrontation only in criminal prosecutions, and did not extend this right to civil proceedings. He would have emphasized that the right of the employer to hire and fire without any stated ground had been generally sustained, in the absence of statute.

Holmes used to tell his secretaries that the only "prime" authority was found first in his opinions in the Supreme Court of the United States; second, in his opinions on the Massachusetts Court; and, of much less importance, in the opinions of his brethren on the United States Court.

He might then have cited his "policeman" decision when he was on the Massachusetts Supreme Court. A policeman was removed from his job by the Mayor of New Bedford for taking an active part in politics in violation of a rule of the police regulations. He claimed that his constitutional right to free speech had been violated. Holmes, dismissing his petition for a mandamus to restore him, remarked that although he might "have a constitutional right to talk politics he has no constitutional right to be a policeman."

He might have added in our supposed case that if Congress believed that the existing procedure was unjust and tended to weaken the protections of civil service, and to discourage men of ability and integrity from joining the government—as would probably have been argued—that was a matter for Congress to correct, not the courts. He would not read into his judgment the protection of the right to confrontation in civil cases not found in the Constitution, or derive it from the vague utterance of due process, any more than, in the child labor cases, he could find no adequate basis at common law, or any clause in the Constitution forbidding Congress to protect children.

I do not suggest that such a decision would have been correct. It is a close question that might go either way. I am describing Holmes's probable approach. Criticism of a decision should be leveled not at the result but at the court's reasoning. A judge's first duty is not to bring about any particular end, whether "good" or "bad," but to apply general rules to particular facts. I suggest that Holmes, if he were today a member of the Supreme Court, would have sided more often with Justice Frankfurter and Justice Harlan than with the "liberal" members of the Court.

THERE IS AN irony behind Holmes's great popularity as a "liberal" judge. It sprang from the fact that he was unwilling to hold certain statutes unlawful which his associates on the bench struck down on the grounds that they offended the loose commands of due process. Few of his admirers took into consideration that in private Holmes was not in sympathy with the social reforms that most of these laws sought to bring about—reforms that expressed the liberal creed of the day. And to the same group, who believed sweepingly in the right to freedom of speech, it does not seem to have occurred that it was Holmes who wrote several opinions which sustained convictions against those who exercised this supposed right. I suspect that the beauty and eloquence of his dissents in the *Abrams* and other cases made the liberals forget this consistent position. They hailed the "clear and present danger" test, but often did not understand it, imagining that it meant danger to the United States, instead of danger that the substantive act would occur that was forbidden by the particular statute.

And it is equally ironical to remember that another famous expression of Holmes—"a dirty business"—used in connection with a case involving wire tapping, should have been so often invoked by those who opposed the practice, when in fact the words were not used by Holmes with reference to the act of tapping a wire, but to the use by the United States of evidence obtained illegally, under a law of the State of Washington which prohibited wire tapping.

The substance of the law, according to Holmes, at any given time pretty nearly corresponds with what is then thought to be "convenient." He constantly recurred to this thought. Since law is but one expression of community life, you must look to the community to discover the existing notions of public policy, which are continually changing. He would not speak of justification, for that presupposed an absolute criterion, whereas the problem was: "Does this decision represent what the lawmaking power must be taken to want?" He would have liked to get a more definite reason than that the decision was in consonance with our sense of justice, and find a more specific policy than that. Law is what the supreme power in the community wills; and all that could be expected from modern improvements is that legislation should easily and quickly, yet not too quickly, modify itself to the will of that *de facto* power, and that the spread of an educated sympathy should reduce the sacrifice of minorities to a minimum.

But even if we reduce our goal for decision to a reliance on our sense of justice, or an examination of what is held to be moral or even convenient by the community, the difficulty in the application of such standards becomes apparent when we look at some of the cases. It is often hard to discover what the community does think.

For instance, the Supreme Court considered whether De George, a bootlegger who didn't pay revenue taxes, should have been deported as an alien who had committed a crime involving "moral turpitude"—the statutory test. The trial court ordered him deported. The majority of the Supreme Court sustained the deportation. Three dissenters, for whom the late Robert H. Jackson spoke, found the definition of moral turpitude unintelligible. He had never discovered, Jackson wrote, that disregard of the nation's liquor taxes excluded a citizen from our best society, and could see no reason why it should banish an alien from our worst. Criminality is one thing—a matter of law; morality, ethics, and religious teaching another, and we tread on treacherous grounds when we undertake to translate ethical concepts into legal ones, case by case.

A similar decision, in the Court of Appeals for the Second

Circuit, in which Judge Learned Hand wrote the opinion, involved the finding whether a man who had petitioned for naturalization, was, in the words of the statute, *a person of good moral character.* Francioso had married his niece in Connecticut, and knew that such a marriage was there considered incestuous and declared a crime. The couple had four children, and lived together in apparent concord. "We can think," wrote Judge Hand, "of no course open to him which would not have been regarded as more immoral than that which he followed, unless it be that he should live at home, but as a celibate. There may be purists who would insist that this alone was consistent with 'good moral conduct'; but we do not believe that the conscience of the ordinary man demands that degree of ascesis; and we have for warrant the fact that the Church —least of all complaisant with sexual lapses—saw fit to sanction the continuance of this union."

Another case in the same circuit dealt with euthanasia. The alien who was petitioning for naturalization had deliberately put to death his son of thirteen by means of chloroform. The child had suffered from his birth a brain injury which made him an idiot and a physical monstrosity—blind, mute, and with all his limbs malformed. He had to be fed; the movements of his bowels and bladder were involuntary; and his life was spent in a small crib. For this murder the father had been convicted and served a prison term. Judge Hand, writing for the court, denied naturalization, but without prejudice to a new petition after the five years required by the statute of "good moral character" after the murder had elapsed. He felt reasonably sure that only a minority of virtuous persons would deem the practice morally justifiable while it remained in private hands.

In a similar case a petitioner was in every way qualified for citizenship, except that, on his own admission, he had now and then engaged in sexual intercourse with unmarried women. Judge Hand, writing for the court, which permitted naturalization, did not see how the judges could get any help from the outside on what the community thought was moral. He suggested that even if a poll could be taken to determine character it would not be enough merely to count heads, without an appraisal of the voters: "A majority of the votes of those in prisons and brothels, for instance, ought scarcely to outweigh the votes of accredited church-goers. Nor can we see any reason to suppose that the opinion of clergymen would be a more reliable estimate than our own."

These cases were recently discussed by Charles P. Curtis, that witty and thoughtful Boston lawyer who died recently, in a book published after his death, which he called *Law as Large as Life.* Now and then he recounts talk worth remembering, particularly a talk that Hand had with Holmes. They jogged down to the Capitol together—it was before the justice had a car, and he was bound for the Court. To tease him into a response, as they parted, Hand said: "Well, sir, goodbye. Do Justice!" The other turned sharply: "That is not my job. My job is to play the game according to the rules."

Hand said he had tried to follow the rules, though oftentimes found that he didn't know what the rules were, for values are incommensurables. You can get a solution only by a compromise, or call it what you will. It must be one that people won't complain of too much; but you cannot expect any more objective measure. . . . He added that physics are apparently also *very shifty.* Heisenberg,* one of the top men, said: "There ain't no rules in this game. An electron may make up its mind to go backward or any other way. It is all a question of statistics." Hand said he felt that way sometimes when he heard about the eternal principles of jurisprudence; of course, you have got to have in your society some at least provisional but authoritative compromises, some tentative solutions—and by "authoritative" he meant compromises that had

---

* Werner Heisenberg, a famous German physicist and Nobel prize winner.

sanctions. The most that you can ask is that they shall be likely to secure assent and not provoke resistance. He meant by "law" those adjustments which will be most likely to be accepted for a *period that you needn't now look beyond.*

ONE OF THE two laymen who spoke at the Marshall conference was Samuel Hutchison Beer, Chairman of the Department of Government at Harvard. Perhaps because he was not a lawyer, was not subject to the sleepy self-intoxication of legal platitudes, his approach was refreshing in its simplicity and common sense. Law and moral insight, Beer said, continually conflict. Is there any other social activity that ought to be under a government of laws and not men? Do parents ever frame a satisfactory rule as to whether their small boy should or should not fight, or when their teen-age daughter had to get in after her date? —a real rule, without bogus escape clauses like "reasonableness." In so many occasions the legal rule did not cover the case; or when it did, logically speaking, it would have been unjust or impracticable to apply the rule. Perhaps unique situations—in law, where two important values conflict—must be dealt with by evaluations not logically derived from the book, or even in conflict with those that are. Why should those in the administration of justice try to eliminate the element of art, of personal judgment, of imaginative insights, and hold only to the spirit of the law, often so hostile from a common-sense point of view, to the task before them? The rule of law itself need not, and does not always exclude the rule of men—the power of pardon, for instance. And this teacher of history added a few words from Plato: "The differences of men and actions, and the endless irregular movements of human things, do not admit of any universal and simple rule; and no art, whatsoever, can lay down a rule which will last for all time."

If such "personalism" (to use Beer's word) runs the risk of permitting judges to write their prejudices into an opinion, it also permits the use of moral sensitivity in the broadest sense, what Justice Holmes called *aperçues,* something deeper and subtler than the reaches of logic. Beer's suggestion is of course no guide for decision, but should not be ignored in keeping the intelligence free from the mechanism of rules and formulas, and the block of absolutes. Since we are forced to conclude that courts are called upon to make value judgments, without the constraint of too rigid formula, it is not without interest to reflect that there are other areas in which such a power is exercised. We must not get away too far from life, and should continually touch the earth for renewed vitality.

I SUGGEST THAT the conference in so far as it was concerned with finding the guiding "principles" that should establish or even suggest the *ratio decidendi* came out about where Holmes began some eighty years ago. As lawyers we have come to recognize that the only thing that is eternal in our world is change, and to discard the warnings of the past in favor of sharper instruments and more revealing intuitions. Having abandoned long ago the quest for the grail, Holmes found it unnecessary to invoke the shop-worn generalities of the past, scattered in the lawbooks. They did not help him in construing statutes; in the nice balancing of authority between the rewards of the shrewd and strong and the needs of the average and the weak; in determining when language turns from persuasion to unlawful incitement; in putting a finger on the point where freedom to proselytize may be treated as a nuisance under the police power, or a trespass on the right of the individual to some privacy.

About such pious handwritings on the wall of time, Judge Hand, whose vision was level with Holmes's, in prose as plucked and lambent as that of the older man, but clearer and less elliptical, and addressed to a wider audience, has this to say: "These stately admonitions refuse to subject themselves to analysis. They are precipitates of 'old, unhappy, far-off things and battles long ago,' originally cast as universals to enlarge the scope of the victory, to give it authority, to reassure the very victors themselves that they have been champions in something more momentous than a passing struggle. Thrown large upon the screen of the future as eternal verities, they are emptied of the vital occasions which gave them birth and become moral adjurations, the more imperious because inscrutable, but with only that content which each generation must pour into them anew in the light of its own experience. If an independent judiciary seeks to fill them from its own bosom, in the end it will cease to be independent."

Justice Holmes and Judge Hand are both religious skeptics. Like all those who cannot accept the comfort of theological revelation, and have committed themselves to doubt rather than to faith, they did so, not because they believed they could demonstrate the correctness of their unbelief, but because in the impossibility of knowledge they were morally and aesthetically more convinced by the vision of man, standing without illusion, without fear, without guilt, to face with dignity and courage the unknown.*

Where are we left?

---

* Lee R. V. Sampson, Lecturer at the University of Bristol, in *Entering an Age of Crisis: The Limits of Religious Thought: The Theological Controversy,* from which this language is taken.

FELIX FRANKFURTER in an admirable little book about Justice Holmes, published three years after his death,* spoke of Holmes's "organic philosophy," which made him realize that while principles gain significance through application, concrete instances are inert except when galvanized into life by a general principle. Because I have emphasized, perhaps unduly, Holmes's skepticism and his distrust of all generalities, I do not wish to imply that he did not have a philosophy about his work. He would have denied that it involved cosmic significance, or that he indulged in a philosophic system, and would have limited his basic beliefs of what was the proper role of the judge, and his view of the Constitution, to the passing reality of the here and the now.

Holmes's view of the Constitution was that its provisions are "not mathematical formulas having their essence in their form; [but] organic living institutions transplanted from English soil. Their significance is vital not formal; it is to be gathered not simply by taking the words and a dictionary, but by considering their origin and their line of growth."

Contrast this way of thinking with what the Supreme Court said when it voided the Agricultural Adjustment Act in 1936. All that was required, according to Justice Owen J. Roberts, speaking for the majority, was "to lay the article of the Constitution which is invoked beside the statute which is challenged and to decide whether the latter squares with the former." The comparison shows the immense importance of a judge's basic conception of what the Constitution is. To Holmes it was organic and alive; to Roberts formal and literal.

* *Mr. Justice Holmes and the Supreme Court.*

Thus it is important that a judge should have a clear appreciation of the nature of his function—which, since it is so often unavoidably legislative in effect, should, for that reason particularly, be free of economic or "moral" slants. He should see our modern highly technological and industrialized society as it actually functions. Holmes's understanding of that society came not from personal experience. Essentially he was a philosopher, interested in the "ultimate issues of the destiny of man"—as Frankfurter observed. Yet, withdrawn from the conflicts and clashes of the tough American life of the period, he realized what the struggles represented and what the issues were about with a deeper and more informed understanding than most of his associates on the Court. He knew, for instance, and had known ten years before being appointed to the Massachusetts Supreme Court, that the tacit assumption of the solidity of the interests of society was very common, but believed it to be false. He observed that much or all legislation was class legislation, so that it could not be condemned because it favored one class at the expense of another.

Legislation was empirical, and was, necessarily, the means by which a body having the power shifted its disagreeable burdens to the shoulders of somebody else.* Holmes took into account the modern disposition of economic forces. Of course, economics and law were not the same, but he suspected that the clue to legal doctrine lay in the economic field.

OUR IDEAL JUDGE will distrust phrases, particularly those that are tinctured with a moral flavor, for, as Holmes knew, we are apt to call "that conduct moral about whose

* I am paraphrasing Holmes's language in "The Gas Stoker's Strike," an article that he published in 1873.

effect upon our common interest we have unusually strong convictions." On the bench he should disregard, so far as humanly possible, the dictates of his own creeds; try to understand and respect those of others; and remain sensitive to the need for experiment. Conceiving it to be his duty not to choose between conflicting views and take sides, even if he has strong personal feelings about the issue before him, he will act with moderation. He will be loyal to his conception of the American feeling for the decencies of life, just as Justice Holmes, skeptical as he was about the eternal existence of any code of living, was devoted to his country, both in sustaining its power and in evoking its ideology. Our judge must sense that unity between citizens which recognizes their common aspirations. They are not eternal, but they are ours.